EMOTIONS:

AN INSTRUCTION MANUAL

How to learn to understand, recognize and express your emotions

NIOZA HUBANOVA

Emotions: An Instruction Manual/ Nioza Hubanova – 2024

"Emotions: An Instruction Manual" is a book that will open your understanding of yourself from the first page.
After reading this book, your life will change because you will discover:
- Where your emotions come from and how your brain works
- How to identify and express your emotions in a healthy way
- How to communicate with people so that to be heard
- How to stop fighting with yourself and instead learn to accept and manage your states
- How to change the beliefs that limit you to be yourself and live a fulfilling life.

Copyright © 2024 Nioza Hubanova

All rights reserved.

No portion of this book may be reproduced in any form without written permission from the author, except as permitted by U.S. copyright law.

For permission requests, contact the author, Nioza Hubanova:

ISBN: 979-8-9917-2221-6 (paperback),

ISBN: 979-8-9917222-0-9 (hardback),

Book Cover by @germancreative

2024

Thank you. The book changed my life overnight. I discovered such a cocktail of feelings, emotions, and experiences within myself that I felt like I grew at least twice in one night.

I matured, aged, and then returned to childhood. A newfound interest in life as a whole appeared, particularly in observing my life.

Svitlana Rohosenko

Feelings, situations... Your book completely transformed my perspective on EMOTIONS. I always believed there were bad and good feelings, and I would suppress them unconditionally, without even thinking about it, because I didn't know there was another way. I used to wonder why I kept getting ill, especially after arguments or stressful situations. Now, I listen to myself and I hear completely different things than I've been imposed upon, and that brings me great joy, gives me strength and energy. Thank you once again for this book.

Olexandra Brin

I really liked your book; I'm rereading it for the countless time.

Some people turn to the Bible in difficult situations, but for me, your book is my Bible. I am very grateful for your book; it is truly a "Beginner's Guide".

I haven't come across any psychology books that are as easy to understand and read. In one word — it is a masterpiece. Thank you!

Svitlana Tarasevych

The book I had the opportunity to read is an essential resource for anyone striving to better understand their emotions, learn to recognize, experience, and express them in a healthy way. The author highlights key aspects of emotional literacy, providing readers with concrete tools to enhance emotional intelligence.

The core idea of the book is that emotions are a natural part of human life, and understanding their essence can significantly improve the quality of our existence. The author distinguishes between "controlling" and "managing" emotions: the former exhausts us, while the latter helps us grow. Emphasis is placed on the idea that emotions should neither be suppressed nor shamed, as this can lead to inner conflicts and even psychosomatic illnesses.

The book's key points include:

- <u>Localization of Emotions in the Brain.</u> The author explains that emotions are formed in the limbic system of the brain. For example, fear and anger are activated in the amygdala, while joy involves the hippocampus and prefrontal cortex. This demonstrates that emotions have a biological basis rather than being abstract or random reactions.
- <u>Primary and Secondary Emotions.</u> The book differentiates between primary emotions (e.g., anger, joy, fear, disgust) and secondary emotions (e.g., shame about feeling shame or guilt about anger). Secondary emotions develop under the influence of social environments, including upbringing.
- <u>Recognizing Emotions.</u> Skills for recognizing emotions are presented as the first step toward emotional self-regulation. Readers are encouraged to keep an emotion journal to track connections between emotions, thoughts, situations, and reactions.
- <u>Understanding Emotions.</u> The author offers a method for linking emotions to specific situations, thoughts, and behaviors, helping to prevent unconscious reactions.
- <u>Expressing Emotion.</u> Healthy ways of expressing emotions are described, including non-verbal methods (gestures, facial expressions), verbal methods (using words), and actions. Particular importance is given to "I-messages" (e.g., "I feel angry when..."), which help avoid conflicts.

The material is presented in a structured way, with tasks and examples emphasizing the book's practical focus. Exercises for self-observation, such as body scanning or keeping an emotion journal, are particularly valuable.

The strengths and advantages of the book include:
- <u>Simplicity of Presentation:</u> The author avoids excessive academic language, making the book accessible to a wide audience.
- <u>Practical Value:</u> The methods and exercises can be immediately applied in daily life.
- <u>Focus on Growth:</u> Readers are encouraged not to avoid emotions but to embrace them as part of themselves.

It is worth noting that for readers already familiar with the concepts of emotional intelligence, the material may seem somewhat basic. Additionally, the book could include more information on the social context of emotions, such as how they influence group dynamics or professional environments. However, it is clear that covering these areas was not the purpose of this work and might be addressed in the author's future publications.

This book can undoubtedly be recommended:
- To those who want to better understand their emotions and learn to manage them.
- To individuals interested in psychology and self-awareness.
- To parents who wish to help their children understand emotions.

In summary, the book's greatest strength is that it offers readers simple and effective tools for working with emotions. It serves as a helpful guide for those seeking emotional balance and harmonious relationships with themselves and others.

Olena Buhachevska

PhD in Psychology, HGEU Professor.
Psychological Counseling and Training Practice Since 1997.
Active in Scientific Research Since 2006.
Author of Over 30 Scientific Works, Including Three Monographs

EMOTIONS:
AN INSTRUCTION MANUAL

NIOZA HUBANOVA

CONTENTS

About the Author   1

Introduction   7

Chapter 1 – Where Do Our Emotions Live?   11

Chapter 2 – Secondary Emotions   17

Chapter 3 – How Do You Distinguish Emotions?   21

Chapter 4 – How To Recognize Your Emotions?   41

Chapter 5 - How To Express Your Emotions?   51

Chapter 6 - Conscious Processing Of Emotions   63

Afterword   75

ABOUT THE AUTHOR

Nioza Hubanova is a well-known Ukrainian Psychologist and Gestalt Therapist whose professional path is closely related to self-knowledge and helping other people solve their psychological problems. Since childhood, Nioza has had a special interest in the human psyche. At the age of four, she had her first consultation with a Psychologist, which was the first step in her long and difficult path of self-development and self-discovery. Even then, she began to think about how the world and people work, and it was these thoughts that led her to a profession that has become a true life's work.

However, the path to professional success was not easy. Having gone through personal psychological crises, including depression, panic attacks and suicidal thoughts, codependent relationships, and much more, Nioza found the strength to overcome these challenges. She didn't stop after unsuccessful attempts to find a qualified Psychotherapist, and eventually, her life has changed thanks to Gestalt therapy. This method helped her not only to overcome her own difficulties but also to open up new opportunities for professional development.

Since 2018, Hubanova has been actively practicing, working both individually and in group formats. She is also the author of the book "Emotions: An Instruction Manual", which has been acknowledged by colleagues and clients for highlighting important aspects of self-regulation and emotional maturity. Besides, Nioza organises numerous workshops, courses and therapy groups on emotional intelligence, psychological healing and couple relationships. The main idea of Nioza's work is to help people with self-knowledge, development of their emotional competence, and create a space where everyone can find support and feel the inner strength for change. Over the years of her practice, she has helped hundreds of clients find answers to difficult questions about themselves, the world, and their relationships with others.

Nioza is an active participant in the Ukrainian psychological community and regularly gives speeches at conferences, particularly at the Interregional Institute of Gestalt Therapy and Art (MIGIS), where she conducts training for future Gestalt Therapists. Her activity covers not only therapeutic practice but also the creation of training programs and marathons that promote development of personal potential of beginner Psychologists.

Currently, Nioza Hubanova continues to actively work on new projects directed towards supporting the psychological health of Ukrainians, especially during the difficult times of war. She believes that everyone has the potential for healing and growth, and her mission is to help people find this resource within themselves.

She constantly deepens her knowledge and practical skills. Her learning and development take place not only through classical education, but also through active participation in various projects, seminars and workshops. Over the past few years, from 2019 to 2024, Nioza has participated in numerous educational and professional events directed towards developing her own practice and providing support to other Psychologists and clients.

Nioza made her first significant steps toward professional development in 2019. She launched several group projects, including "Psychology of Dreams", where she helped people analyse their dreams, which became an important tool for self-knowledge. At the same time, she worked on the development of emotional intelligence in a group format, conducting seminars and projects on topic "Emotional Intelligence".

Another significant project was "Psychology of Overweight", implemented in cooperation with a Nutritionist. This project was dedicated to the study of the psychological causes of overweight, which allowed her to help many clients comprehend the connection between emotional state and eating habits. At the same time, Nioza created a useful resource for beginner Psychologists — a checklist to help them start their practice effectively.

2020 became a remarkable year in Nioza's career thanks to the publication of the book "Emotions. An Instruction Manual", which has become an important tool for many people striving to better understand and manage their emotions. Furthermore, Nioza has conducted a number of educational projects and courses. There are a marathon "Self-Esteem", a course "Mindfulness", and a project "Everything is in Your Hands" among them, dedicated to self-regulation and emotion management.

Thanks to active cooperation with the Interregional Institute of Gestalt Therapy and Art (MIGIS), she took part in a conference with a workshop on topic "Mythopoetic World of Trauma", where she deepened her knowledge of traumatic experience and its impact on the human psyche.

2021 brought new opportunities for Nioza's professional development, especially in the context of working with interpersonal relationships. At the MIGIS conference, she presented a workshop called "Offences in a Couple" dedicated to resolving conflicts in relationships. Simultaneously, she became a trainee of the first educational degree group of Gestalt therapy training in Odesa, where she taught a new generation of Therapists the fundamentals of this methodology.

In 2022, due to the war in Ukraine, Nioza launched new projects directed towards supporting Ukrainians during these difficult times. She created a course "Healing of a Trauma", which helped many people process difficult emotional worries through therapeutic support groups. She also conducted several workshops on psychotherapeutic practice and helping Psychologists in developing their professional skills.

2023 was full of new workshops and research, including on the topic of impact of social media on psychotherapy. Nioza has created several educational webinars, including a free webinar on ethics for Psychologists. She also actively worked on the development of training groups on Gestalt therapy in online format. Participation in international conferences, such as the MIGIS conference with the workshop "Safety Lives in Your Body", allowed her to expand her audience and share her experience with colleagues.

For 2024, Nioza has planned many new initiatives, including individual mentoring for Psychologists, which will help specialists develop and improve their qualification. A webinar on social media ethics, intervision groups and therapy groups are also important aspects of her plans for the future. In addition, Nioza is working on creating a team of Psychologists, which opens up new prospects for professional development and cooperation.

Thus, Nioza Hubanova's path is a vivid example of continuous development, deep interest in profession and an unwavering strive to enhance her knowledge and skills directed towards helping others. Her numerous projects, workshops, and educational programs have made a significant contribution to the psychological community, and her influence continues to grow every year.

INTRODUCTION

This book is written to explain in an easy and accessible way what emotions are, what types of emotions there are, and how to understand, recognize and express them.

Emotional self-regulation skills are fundamentally important and affect quality of our life.

Imagine you have been given powerful tools to understand yourself and the world, but no one has taught you how to use them. Drawing an analogy with emotions, they are something that comes naturally to us, and it is supposed to be the parents or guardians who teach us how to understand them.

But what if the parents themselves do not quite understand what is going on inside them, do not know how to distinguish one emotion from another, do not know how to manage them?

Then it turns out that emotions live separately: you feel something, but you do not understand what it is, and from this you may get scared, be anxious, trying to get rid of them.

Indeed, human's natural reactions to internal and external factors will not go anywhere and will continue to affect you in the same way. Without bringing them into the scope of recognition, you will not be able take the charge into your own hands.

The constant resistance and desire to control your thoughts and emotions, instigate suffering, you become hostage to this limited perception.

I want to immediately distinguish between the terms control and manage.

The first one is about what I try to prevent, suppress and hold the inevitable.

The second is about what I notice, recognize, accept, and choose where to direct that energy.

In the first case, you spend a tremendous amount of your mental energy on, essentially meaningless actions, because has there ever been a time when you managed to quickly suppress an emotion and then it never manifested again?

Everything that is being held back only becomes a ticking time bomb, eventually exploding with unpleasant consequences, either internally, destroying you from within, or externally, destroying everything around you.

What would happen if we learnt to recognize and express emotions?

This means you will no longer have to eat up stress, fall into panic attacks, fear losing your mind, force your body to "hurt", dissolve into others, or live someone else's life.

By enhancing level of your emotional intelligence, you improve the quality of your own life.

I would like to point out that this is not about you never suffering, always being calm and happy, it is, in the main, about everything being the same, but your perception being different!

Recognizing an emotion helps you to process it, meaning it will be a natural process that is not draining and exhausting, but fulfilling and enriching.

You will understand the causes and factors that affect the occurrence of emotions within you, which will help you make better sense of yourself and how to act in your life.

You will be able to choose what to embrace and what to let go of, what you want and what you don't, as well as where your personal boundaries lie and where others' boundaries are.

You will finally gain the ability to clearly express your desires and satisfy your needs.

Another important message in this book lies in blurring of rigid boundaries between a "good" and a "bad" emotion. This perspective may be completely new to you, but it will expand your perception and free you from swinging from one extreme to another.

CHAPTER 1
WHERE DO OUR EMOTIONS LIVE?

Emotions are a realm of our psyche, reflecting how we respond to internal and external changes.

There is the limbic system in our brain, which is the home of our emotions.

This system scans everything around us for danger, thereby keeping us safe at all times. Brain detects an impetus and sends information about it to our body, prompting a respond – this is how an emotion is born.

Feelings of fear and rage are born in the amygdala, an element of the limbic system, and are activated when a person sees food, a sexual partner, enemies and so on.

The feeling of being stalked by someone when walking down the street at night is also work of the amygdala bodies.

Surprisingly, rage is similar to happiness – it pushes us forward in the same way that joy and pleasure do, but fear and anxiety force us, conversely, to pull away.

In a state of fury, rage, various areas of our brain are activated, because we need to assess the situation, refer to memory, experience, to produce the appropriate hormones – to fully prepare our organism for a certain feeling.

Feelings of joy, laughter are born in the hippocampus, amygdales, prefrontal cortex, while guilt and shame are born in the temporal lobes, anatomically these two emotions are adjacent.

Now we know that our sensations do not appear from anywhere; they have a precise location, live in our brain, perform tremendous work every second, have causes, and manifest in specific ways.

Emotions perform 3 main functions:

Signaling.

When events happen around us, that our brain perceives as unfavorable, corresponding emotions are born to make us to act on these sensations. For example, if an event threatens our safety, we understand we should run, whereas if an event suggests pleasure, we begin to move closer.

Regulatory.

Emotions help regulate our internal tension so that we stay balanced rather than burned out or exhausted.

By paying attention to our needs, we can stick to the path we need. Thus, emotions regulate our lives, encouraging us to take these or those actions.

Communicative.

We broadcast our inner world to others through the expression of emotions. This way the people around us can understand how we feel, what our desires are, and how to interact with us. By reacting to the words and actions of other people, we give them feedback about themselves, enabling them to adjust and regulate their behavior to help us connect and grow closer.

This is why it is so important to express our emotions in order to build relationships with people.

There are basic emotions – these are the most fundamental emotions that cannot be broken down into anything simpler.

Anger

Sadness

Fear (anxiety)

Disgust

Joy

Interest

Surprise

Tenderness

Gratitude

Satisfaction

Shame and guilt are also considered basic, although they contain rage, directed at oneself and fear of losing the approval of others.

We will highlight some of them with you.

What does each of these emotions tell us?

Anger (irritation, rage, fury, hatred, resentment) – tells that our personal boundaries are being violated, needs are not being satisfied, there is a need to protect something valuable, to express ourselves.

Sadness (sorrow, longing, melancholy, grief) – tells us of bereavement, of losing something valuable, resources, of ending a relationship, of saying goodbye and accepting reality.

Shame (embarrassment, confusion, shyness) and Guilt – tells us that we have done something wrong, stumbled, made a mistake, and it's best not to do it again in the future.

Fear (anxiety, fright, panic, apprehension) – tells us of danger, of something destructive and harmful, of the strive to avoid it, as well as warns us of potential violations of our boundaries.

Disgust (revulsion, disdain, aversion) – tells that we need to reject something unpleasant, push it away, leave it behind, and forget about it.

Joy – tells that something important and valuable is happening right now, and this process needs to be maintained, strengthened, approached.

Interest – tells of discovery, revealing and changing of something new, of approach, contact.

As you can see, all these emotions are useful and necessary; they were not simply instilled in us by nature for any reason. Therefore, when we try to suppress or *control* them, we only make it worse for ourselves, as we cannot rid of them. And by suppressing their manifestation, we put our existence at a great risk.

It is also important to identify the intensity of our emotions so that we can manage them. When the intensity peaks, a risk of not being able to handle the emotion appears, which can cause it manage you.

The intensity can be *low* (1-3 points), *moderate* (4-7 points), or *high* (7-10 points). If the intensity of the emotion peaks, it can turn out either in the body as a psychosomatic illness or to a state of shock.

CHAPTER 2

SECONDARY EMOTIONS

From the previous chapter we have learnt what basic emotions are, and they are primary, meaning they are innate, natural. But secondary emotions are learned, those that are formed in the process of upbringing in the family; they also become the causes of our psychological problems.

These include the shame of shame – when we feel ashamed of being able to feel shame; shame of sadness – when we feel ashamed of being sad; guilt over anger – when we feel guilty for being angry; fear of anger – when we are afraid of being able to feel anger; and the shame of joy and love – when we feel ashamed of being joyful and love.

Formation of secondary emotions happens because in childhood our parents did not accept, did not acknowledge, ignored, criticized our basic emotions, forbade to show them, to experience them, shamed, punished us for them, or if there was an unspoken prohibition on any of these emotions in the family.

Parents may have denied your feelings and convinced you of others, thus teaching you to doubt and distrust your feelings.

For example, you might have walked up to them and said, "I'm scared", to which they responded, "No, you're not scared; you shouldn't be afraid". This happens not because your parents are "bad", but because they were raised in the same way. They follow limited beliefs about what is "good" and what is "bad", what you can experience and what you cannot, what society welcomes and what not, what you should be and what you shouldn't be.

We can be raised in such a way as to make us comfortable for our parents, be conformed to their expectations, and don't object, so that we can be controlled.

Desire to control may be linked to their fear of you leaving them and not wanting to be alone. They might not even recognize this need, thinking that they simply want to do what's best for you and care for you. Alternatively, if they don't know how to live their own lives, they may choose to live yours instead.

When this need is managed to be clarified and acknowledged – as it's normal to not desire to be alone and to desire the presence and love of those dear to us – behavior can change. It opens up the chance to discuss it and find new ways to satisfy that need.

Behavior and response patterns, values and goals are reviewed.

So, when parents want to shape certain behavior in you, they cut the emotions they don't like and reinforce the emotions they like.

Example: person who hides his/her "negative" emotions, always joyful, wanting to help, but inside he/she is terribly anxious, very scared, and he/she is on the verge of a breakdown.

This is a case where, from childhood, there's inculcated that crying is not allowed – it's a sign of weakness, and weakness is bad. Asking for help is bad, complaining is bad, feeling sad is not allowed, being angry is not allowed.

However, when you smile and eagerly rush to help, then we love you. If you feel guilt and apologize, then you are good.

This confines us within limits that we remain in until our level of discomfort peaks. At that point, we learn to suppress, hold back, and fight our emotions in order to conform to these "norms".

When we try to communicate our true emotions but they are not noticed, we have to intensify their manifestation to be noticed. This is how we get used to exaggerating emotions – yelling, panicking, self-harming ourselves.

As a result of all the above, the natural chain of reactions – "my need is dissatisfied, so I'm angry" or "I like it, so I do it" – is disrupted.

Because we cannot trust our emotions or lean on them, we begin to rely on the opinions of others, resulting in living a life that isn't truly ours. At the moment when we need to respond to an event, understand whether we like it or not, and decide how to act, we start seeking advice and help, choosing to rely on someone else's experience. This is because we've got used to believe that what we feel is wrong and bad.

Or we try to listen to ourselves, to choose coming from our own senses, but at that moment another person starts telling us how it would be better to act, and we can't withstand his/her pressure, our personal boundaries are easily pushed through, everything feels like it's in a fog, and before we know it, we're doing what we were told.

Inability to establish personal boundaries, protect them, and withstand pressure stems from our failure to distinguish and identify our emotions. We fear them, consider them wrong, and do not rely on them.

Task: write down your "secondary" emotions, for example, "I feel ashamed to cry" or "I'm afraid to be angry". Remember on when these emotions occurred, when you started thinking this way, and perhaps you remember who told you this?

Write down everything that comes to mind regarding this topic. Read it over and identify how you now view these "secondary" emotions, these beliefs. Do you like them? Would you like to change anything about them? If so, what would that be?

CHAPTER 3
HOW DO YOU DISTINGUISH EMOTIONS?

The ability to distinguish your emotions is the first step in forming emotional self-regulation skills.

It's about being able to clearly identify what emotion you're experiencing at the moment and being able to name it.

In infancy, at the age of 8 months, we have only two emotions: like it a lot and dislike it a lot, and from them the basic emotions known to us branch out and form later on.

Our mother teaches us how to distinguish and identify these emotions.

For example, when we hear a loud noise and start crying, our mother says "You're scared". If someone takes our toy, we begin to stomp our feet and cry, and we are told "You are angry right now".

But, as mentioned earlier, if the parents themselves do not know how to distinguish emotions, they will not be able to teach us to do so either.

Then, at an older age, we can learn this ourselves or seek help from a therapist. Otherwise, if we don't establish a connection with our emotions, anxiety will settle within us. We may try to cope by eating up, drinking, drug ourselves, dissolve ourselves in another person, self-harming, attack others, or endlessly seeking a physical reason for this inexplicable feeling inside, but all of it will be in vain.

Next, I will tell you how to start noticing what is happening in your body, how to track your emotions, thoughts, and behavior, establish the cause-and-effect link of their occurrences, and what to do in each individual case.

In fact, a huge resource, your friend and helper, is your body. It can answer many questions that you pose to the external world.

And here's the first question for you: "How often do you pay attention to your physical sensations during different situations?".

So, when you say a certain word or hear it addressed to you, how does your body react in that moment?

Or you might be standing in the kitchen, washing dishes, sitting in a café with a friend, or watching a movie – do you notice what thoughts pass through your mind, and how does your body react to them afterward?

We rarely focus on it because we don't even know how much it's important and useful to us.

I suggest trying it for yourself:

For a week, 3 times a day, at any time and under any circumstances, ask yourself the question, "What am I feeling right now?". Direct your gaze inward, concentrate, analyze each part of your body, and try to understand what you are sensing.

Start with a basic description of your body temperature, the level of tension-relaxation, comfort-discomfort, fatigue-vigor…

By detailing, you will begin to get closer to naming your state – I'm anxious, I'm excited, I'm sad, I'm shy, I'm inspired, I'm joyful.

Thus, you'll make it a habit of observing yourself. With each time, it will become more accessible and easier, enabling you to turn to yourself and rely on yourself whenever necessary.

Before every action, choice, or decision, ask yourself: "Do I want this?" and, following the same pattern, search for the answer within yourself. Start with the routine – what do I want to wear today? What do I want to eat today? What do I want to watch today? Who do I want to spend time with?

Slow down and scan your sensation and then make a decision.

You can also train your sensitivity before sleep:

Relax, immerse yourself in your inner processes, and start from the top of your head. Feel if your mind is tense, if your eyes, neck, and lip muscles are relaxed, and whether you're comfortable in your current position. Pay attention to your neck, shoulders, chest – how your heart is beating, whether it's slow or fast, how you are breathing, and what's happening in your stomach – whether it's calm... In this way, go through your entire body.

If you find unfamiliar worries, discomfort, or something that catches your attention in any area, begin to notice when that sensation intensifies and when it disappears throughout the day.

Let's now talk about each basic emotion in more detail.

Anger

Anger occurs when our need is not satisfied. In other words, we want something but do not receive it. This can occur in situations of lack. For example, if I feel I am not receiving enough attention from a dear person.

Or in a situation of excess – there's too much of that attention.

Feeling of anger can vary in intensity – mild anger is often referred to as irritation, the next level is simply anger, then there's rage, and finally fury. But all of this, regardless of the word, is essentially anger.

Anger signals to us that something is not right, indicating a need to protect ourselves or to make a change.

What happens when we suppress or forbid it?

We deprive ourselves of the ability to notice when our needs are not being satisfied, there is no motivation in us to change anything, we may not notice the danger and we may not distance ourselves from it in time.

Moreover, anger is closely related to our self-expression in the world. If we choose to hold the energy needed for action, everything quiets down along with it.

<u>Any interaction we have with the world is an act of aggression.</u>

You probably have negative associations with the word "aggression", but it's time to expand the perception and borders of the meaning of this term.

Speaking in public, entering into intimate relationships, expressing our opinions, kissing, consuming food – these are all acts of aggression, as we demonstrate ourselves to the world through active interaction.

<u>Aggressive behavior is behavior aimed at satisfying the needs.</u>

There are different manifestations of aggression:

- Actively expressing and stating our needs, taking what we need, and giving others what we consider necessary.

- Passively expressing our needs, meaning not openly talking about them and attempting to satisfy them indirectly — manipulating, sabotaging others' actions to get what we want, devaluing it, and feeling offended.

- The need is expressed and being satisfied.

Clearly expressing our desires and satisfying our needs, standing up for our boundaries while respecting others' boundaries, and having the ability to communicate freely with those we want to and not engage with those we don't want to.

- The object of the meeting the need is being destroyed.

Devaluing people, cutting off communication with important people through scandals, arguments, insults, and other ways to ruin one's life.

- Needs are not being satisfied, but contact is not being broken either.

This manifests as dependent relationships, such as living together with a partner who has a substance dependency.

The most natural response to pain is anger, as it is necessary for destroying the source of that pain.

Fear in the face of danger activates anger for protection.

Often there can be other emotions behind anger — fear, shame, guilt, tenderness, grief, offence, and so on.

For example, when a child goes where he/she isn't allowed, a parent might start shouting and getting angry, even though he/she is actually very scared that something might happen to the child.

Or we may feel a lot of tenderness toward someone who is far away, and we start to feel very angry that we cannot hug him/her and express that tenderness.

Offence is suppressed anger.

If something doesn't go our way, and someone hits a vulnerable point while we don't know how to express our anger, we may manipulate offence to make the other person feel guilty.

Anger is present in different transformations of relationships – approaching, distancing, ending, or starting anew.

Look at how many important functions are performed by an emotion that is labelled as "bad", that we were forbidden to experience in childhood, which society does not welcome, and which we suppress.

<u>Physical manifestations of anger</u> include rapid heartbeat, shallow breathing, clenched fists, tight jaw, and a feeling of increased muscle tension.

<u>Situations:</u> your boundaries have been violated, you haven't received what you wanted, or something was done that you didn't want. People are angry with you, shouting, and making claims. Something you want has been taken from you.

<u>Behavior:</u> the urge to shout, curse, hit the person, break something, run away, slam a door.

<u>Thoughts:</u> we are good, the other one is bad.

Sadness

Sadness helps us to mark the end of an important stage in our lives – such as finishing school, moving to a new place, change of co-workers, or ending a relationship.

Sadness is the energy for completing the process of bereavement or loss. In this process, we say goodbye to what was before and smoothly move to a new reality, preserving integrity. In acknowledging sadness, sorrow, we also acknowledge our own helplessness, emptiness, pain...

When we try to bypass this state, we don't allow the process to complete, meaning that the emptiness is either filled with new expectations, illusions, and fantasies, or it is denied.

At this moment, we deprive ourselves of the ability to prepare for and enter into new connections. By blocking sadness, we stop experiencing other emotions as well, causing a sense of emptiness and boredom, resulting in silence.

If in childhood we heard phrases, and continue to hear them today, such as "Don't be sad, don't cry, don't get upset, don't worry, think of something good!" it means we learned not to process this emotion but to suppress it.

When we were distracted with a new toy if the old one broke, when no one sat with us, hugged us, or offered to "be sad together", it means we learned to bypass that feeling.

Or our sadness was devalued with phrases like, "What good are tears? What's the point of being sad?" Now we repeat these phrases to ourselves and others.

The natural flow of worries is anxiety caused by a change in the usual state, followed by rage, which may eventually give way to other feelings, excitement, and activity aimed at changing circumstances. And only completing this series of emotions, sadness serves as a symbol of bereavement.

It's surprising, but the prohibition on sadness can lead to depression and apathy, where I feel nothing, want nothing, and have no life within me – I'm empty. Acknowledging sadness is the first step toward healing.

By not allowing sadness to live its cycle, we don't let it go; instead, we get stuck in it and carry that state with us throughout our lives.

<u>Physical manifestations</u>: fatigue, complete lack of energy, weakness, drowsiness, tearfulness, a lump in the throat, a heaviness in the chest, emptiness in the soul, a nagging longing, and low muscle tone.

<u>Situations</u>: when we have lost or bereaved something that was important to us, breakup, separation, loss of a job, loss of money, or loss of illusions. We are tired and lost emotional resources – it's time to rest.

<u>Behavior</u>: passivity.

<u>Thoughts</u>: we are bad, the world is bad, everything will be bad. A total feeling of hopelessness and a pessimistic view of the world.

Fear

Fear is the knowledge of a destructive past and the strive to avoid similar in the future. It distances us from danger, destroys unfavorable contact, and prevents us from approaching new that may carry potential risks.

It's a simultaneous desire to get to know the new and to run away from it. The energy of fear encourages us to mobilize our resources and change the situation that the feeling triggers, but it can also stop us. We desire to get rid of it, suppressing it and pushing it deep down. However, since it is a basic emotion, it doesn't go away; instead, it starts to act from within, leading to unpleasant consequences.

Fear performs a fundamentally important function – it protects us.

We cannot escape or eliminate it; we can only create the illusion of fearlessness, which is referred to as repression.

Remember when we talked about secondary emotions? Initially, we may not realize we are experiencing fear as it might be masked by guilt, shame, or anger.

Knowing that being afraid is shameful, bad, or wrong, we will blame and shame ourselves for it, which complicates the identification of the original feeling. If we believe that being afraid is a sign of weakness, we will become angry with ourselves, or, upon feeling fear, we may immediately go on the offensive.

The recognition that we have the right to be afraid, just like any living being on this planet, and that this does not make us any worse, frees us from the prohibition on fear. This allows us to access the source of our fear, which we can then work with directly.

I want to clarify the differences between anxiety and fear.

Fear is "objectified"; it relates to a specific object, is defined, and is clear, meaning we can name exactly what we are afraid of.

Anxiety is about the unknown, the undefined, the non-existent, and the imagined. It is usually about the future with thoughts like "What if...?" or the past with "What would have happened if...?".

Fear of something new is a perfectly natural feeling, while where we experience anxiety, there is often interrupted excitement.

<u>Physical manifestations:</u> tremors, shaking, uncontrolled muscle tension, intrusive thoughts, headaches, tearfulness, and rapid heartbeat.

<u>Situations:</u> we are faced with something unfamiliar that we believe we won't handle well. Or an event happens that ended negatively in the past.

<u>Behavior:</u> we complain, cry, ask for help, or avoid the situation. We may fall into perfectionism, desire to prepare as thoroughly as possible to handle the situation.

<u>Thoughts:</u> I won't cope with it, I won't succeed, I will be rejected, I can't do it.

We feel small, weak, and helpless. Meanwhile, we make the situation seem the opposite – grand and overwhelming.

Shame

This feeling is about rejecting ourselves or some part of ourselves. This happens when, in childhood, we were rejected or ignored, inculcated that we are "bad", with the main message being "you are bad". A sense of being "different", "wrong", "flawed". To avoid rejection from parents, a child may be willing to destroy his/her true self and create a false self that will be pleasing to others. Shame involves a constant self-assessment of how one should be and how one shouldn't be, what I deserve and what I don't, and whether I conform the society.

If our parents criticized, humiliated, ignored, or rejected us, we later become that figure for ourselves – we shame ourselves. This is the fear of being genuine, of being who I truly feel I am. Shame strikes at our core, our essence.

Each of us experiences shame to some extent, and it can also be expressed in the opposite way – through the showing of our flaws, indifference, excessive pride, or complete denial of shame.

Suppressed by shame, we try in every way to hide it, holding back our emotions and not articulating our thoughts, because "world" may ridicule, attack, humiliate, or hurt. It's difficult for us to open up to another person, show our true selves, and trust, that is why we often keep others at a distance.

When there is a lot of our own shame, we may experience shame for others, such as when, for instance, someone sings, dances, expresses his/her feelings, or makes a mistake.

Shame shields us from contact, makes us overcautious and second-guess others, thinking they will assess, criticize, or disdain us. Rage can mask shame as a protective mechanism; when we are criticized, assessed, we can become very wrathful while feeling shame.

Because we reject ourselves or parts of ourselves, we lose our own integrity. The world becomes broken into "good" and "bad". Inner unfreedom instigates intense tension, self-rejection, low self-esteem and socialization, limitations in self-expression.

Shame can also serve as a marker that we are doing something uncommon, pushing beyond our limits, and in this way, it brings us back to ourselves.

Physical manifestations: blushing, numbness, a wandering gaze, and the desire to sink through the floor, disappear.

Situations: acted "badly" or "incorrectly", receiving no praise from others, not being approved, rejected or reacted negatively.

Behavior: desire to apologize, ask for forgiveness, or hide and withdraw.

Thoughts: "I am bad", "I am worthless", "I am awful", "others as good and right, yet critical and rejecting towards us".

Guilt

Guilt differs from shame in that it involves assessing our actions – thinking, **"How could I have done THIS?"** – while shame is about assessing ourselves, feeling, "How could I have done this?".

We are told what we can and cannot do, which action is "bad" and which is "good", but how often do you consider who and how decided what is good and what is bad? What criteria are used?

Accordingly, we were raised in a way that suited our parents, and if we didn't listen to them, we were blamed. When something went wrong in our relationships, it was our fault. Guilt was reinforced by constant manipulations like, "When you don't listen to me, it makes me feel bad", or "You didn't bring Dad his glasses on time, and now he's angry."

Such phrases, as if artificially, expand our scope of responsibility to include things that we don't really have to be responsible for. Later, when we see someone is in a bad mood, we immediately take responsibility for it and feel guilty, because we got used to that we are responsible for feelings of others – our actions define their mood.

Guilt is expressed in constant thoughts of "if only I could change everything…". It is about a desire to control – to go back and redo things, and an inability to accept reality, the present, and to forgive oneself. Sometimes, the feeling of guilt helps not to process bereavement, grief, or loss: as long as I think that I am to blame, it means that, presumably, there's still something to change, I can fix everything, and things will go back to how they were; it's going to get better…

When I accept reality and forgive myself, I let go of the situation and, along with it, the person.

This is all a description of neurotic guilt, but it's also important to note about this feeling that, to a rational extent, it is useful: we understand what we did wrong and avoid repeating it in the future. Such guilt serves as a compass in society as it helps us understand what we shouldn't do. It performs a regulatory function, helps us follow moral principles and arrangements.

Physical manifestations: a heavy feeling in the chest, dispiritedness, tension, shortness of breath, and rapid heartbeat.

Situations: I made a mistake, acted badly, others reacted negatively.

Behavior: a desire to apologize or withdraw, self-condemnation.

Thoughts: I acted badly, if only I could have done things differently, turned back time.

Disgust

Disgust signals to us that there is an excess of something unpleasant, and we need to get rid of it.
First, irritation appears, and if it is ignored, it can escalate into disgust, which may be felt as nausea and a desire to reject.
This feeling enables to avoid spoiled or dangerous food, infections, parasites, and also toxic people.
Disgust can occur when our boundaries are violated, when we "eat up and don't digest" offences, beliefs; tolerate and suppress what we dislike within ourselves.
Prohibition on this feeling may form because when a child spits out

food, tells that he/she dislikes certain clothes, or refuses to kiss certain people, he/she is scolded for it.

Thus, child understands that it's wrong to do that and gets used to tolerate or block this feeling and as a sequence, doesn't know how to feel a comfortable distance, his/her boundaries, which is where the merge comes from.

When something is unpleasant in a relationship, he/she may feel guilty for his/her disgust; he/she chooses to suppress it rather than speaks out and regulates it, will tolerate and suffer.

Since disgust helps us identify toxic people, by repressing it, we won't be able to identify what is right for us and what isn't; we wouldn't be able to end an unfavorable relationship.

Repressed feeling of disgust may manifest as physical nausea or vomiting, giving the impression that we have been poisoned. However, in reality, it is about the toxic relationship that is poisoning us.

<u>Physical manifestations:</u> nausea, vomiting, a lump in the throat, malaise, and dispiritedness.

<u>Situation:</u> something bothers us, is disgusting, is unpleasant, or does not correspond with our tastes.

<u>Behavior:</u> a desire to walk away and have nothing to do with it.

<u>Thoughts:</u> I am good, this is disgusting.

Joy

Joy is the energy that is born within us, and we radiate it into the world, sharing something valuable and important.

This emotion helps us identify what we like and what satisfies our needs, it encourages us to approach the source of our joy, fill our connection and reinforcing, supporting it.

Thanks to joy, we take credit for our achievements, process our sense of belonging, and live in the "here and now".

Joy can also be processed through aggression. As we know, aggression is not just something terrible and destructive but also a way of demonstration ourselves to the world. Thus, feeling joy, we may act aggressive, active to the world.

In this emotion, we feel complete; a desire to move, create, and have fun appears. Joy is a charge, our resource.

Sometimes, we forbid ourselves to feel joy due to beliefs and memories of past experiences.

For example, we are aware of phrases like "If you laugh too much, you'll end up crying a lot" or "don't be too happy, or you'll cast an evil eye". These beliefs stop and suppress that energy in us.

We take these phrases as truths, without subjecting them to criticism or doubt. However, in reality, there is no logical connection between feeling joy and the idea that it will lead to tears.

It's clear that we are dynamic beings, and only one emotional state does not exist: we might cry now, laugh later, and then something happens, and we cry again.

We try to control our feelings and our life, so we attempt to connect them at least to something, create consistency and predict the future. In doing so, we deprive ourselves of the ability to feel joy, fully process all our emotions, not getting stuck in them or deform them.

By opening the flow of joy, we enrich ourselves with this important emotion and can recharge and fill ourselves to keep moving forward.

<u>Physical manifestations:</u> a feeling of energy, a surge of strength, vitality, a desire to do something, pleasant muscle tone, a sense of jubilation in the chest, and a wish to laugh and hug everyone.

<u>Situation:</u> we have achieved a goal, succeeded at something, we are praised, understood and acknowledged.

<u>Behavior:</u> talkativeness, we're at our best, we're rushing along [1], we're smiling, wanting to be around people and share these positive emotions with them.

<u>Thoughts:</u> I am strong, special, and awesome; others are good, understanding, acknowledging, and loving.

Interest

Interest promotes our development; it is the energy of searching,

---

[1] *in a slang context, this expression usually means that a person is experiencing strong emotions, which can be both positive (such as joy or excitement) and negative (like sadness or tension). It can also mean that a person is "drifting off" into their thoughts or dreams, as if they are losing touch with reality.*
This phrase is often used to emphasise that a person is deeply engaged in something, and it has a significant impact on them.

discovery, getting close, and cognition.

When we are small, it is interest and curiosity that drive us – to grab this, to climb there.

In adult life, this emotion is just as important; we can process it as excitement – interest in another person or phenomenon. It creates a space for experimentation and gaining experience.

Sometimes, adults forbid us from experimenting and trying, shielding us from new experiences and depriving us of independence. When we ask them about life, they often ignore us or refuse to answer. This frequently happens in questions regarding sex, when a child strives to understand himself/herself, his/her parents, and others, but they get scolded and told that such questions are not to be asked.

They may shield children from various sources of information, even those that are not dangerous or destructive.

Child learns to hold back this energy, becoming non-initiative and disinterested in everything.

It's also important for interest to born naturally, on its own, rather than being artificially created. For example, when a child is forced to be interested in things he/she dislikes, or when there are too many objects piquing his/her interest, and the child no longer responds to stimuli, with everything readily available right in front of him/her.

This also applies to adult life, when everything is already available, there is little reason for interest to born or to motivate us.

The loss of connection with our interest ultimately leads us to questions like **"What do I want from life?"**.

Access to the interest energy is blocked. Curiosity, excitement, and interest are sources of strength and energy.

By the way, fear and interest are related. When we face new experience, we simultaneously fear it and crave it; we feel scared and interested, taking a step back and a step forward, and that's normal too.

Anxiety is interrupted excitement; we either feel anxious or joyful. The ability to manage these energies allows us to live our lives as we desire.

Physical manifestations: slowing down, holding breath and heartbeat in the first seconds, followed by shallow breathing, breathlessness, vibrations in the stomach and chest, an increase in body temperature.

Situation: we are about to encounter a new experience, acquaintance, we want to learn something, test, try, experiment.

Behavior: a desire to explore, to choose this particular activity over another.

Thoughts: "I am interested, this is interesting, unknown, and unfamiliar".

Task for detecting emotions: start a journal where you record your emotions and feelings throughout the day. Try to delve into yourself and identify what emotions you experienced today. If it's difficult at first to clearly name your emotions, describe everything you can: physical sensations, what they feel like, images.
You should write this down every day for 1-2 weeks, so that you can confidently and easily identify your emotional state.

CHAPTER 4
HOW TO RECOGNIZE YOUR EMOTIONS?

Now that we have learned to detect our emotions, identify what we feel, and name them, it's time to learn how to *recognize* them. In this context, recognizing means understanding the causes, connecting the situation-emotion-thought-behavior.

Recognition gives us an ability to manage our emotions before expressing them, choose how we will do so rather than do it automatically.

I'll give an example of emotional overeating, as it happens precisely because we don't track the cause-and-effect link and don't understand whether we are truly hungry or if our needs lie elsewhere.

Situation: you got angry at your boss, habitually held back your rage, came home, and felt a vague emotion – whether it's emptiness, rage, or just a desire to eat... and before you know it, you're bingeing on everything in the fridge, yet satisfaction never comes. This happens because you're trying to satisfy the wrong need. As soon as you walk in the house and feel the urge to eat, slow down and ask yourself: "What am I feeling right now?". Identify the emotion, then ask the next question: "What happened earlier today?". Remember your day and pinpoint the event that led to your emotional state. The third question is: "What do I actually want?" This way, you realize that you don't want to eat but to be angry, hit something, or shout at your boss.

Since we can't always directly implement our desire, it's important to find alternative ways to express one or another emotion. We'll discuss how to express emotions in the next chapter, but for now, your task is to understand the consistent patterns of your reactions and learn to trace the connections.

Another example: you met an interesting person, you liked him/her, you had a great time together, and then came home and felt something strange happening in your body: perhaps tension, a racing heartbeat, and something happening in your stomach...

In that moment, you might feel scared of your emotions, not knowing of what to do with them. However, when you start to concentrate, identify what the emotion is, all the signs come together, and you get excitement, interest!

You remember what happened earlier that might have triggered this emotion, follow the trail back to the memory of your new acquaintance, your meeting, and recognize that this person piqued a lot of interest and excitement in you. And most likely, you want to see his/her again, get closer, and learn more about him/her.

In this case, you won't need to fear or overeat own worries anymore. You'll recognize them, which means you can move on to the next stage – expressing them.

EMOTIONS: AN INSTRUCTION MANUAL

You may notice that the book emphasizes the importance of naturally expressing emotions. But then, why do we need to do all this work to recognize and plan how to express them? Can't we just respond impulsively and spontaneously?

That's correct – the emphasis is on the nature of emotions and their expression.

However, remember that how we respond and behave today is a result of what we were taught in childhood, what we saw, heard, and took over. And as our parents themselves often didn't know and still don't know how to deal with their feelings or express them healthily, so we, in turn, don't know as well.

That's why it's so important to stop yourself, take the time to notice the emotion, its movement, dynamics, and trajectory, and to identify further interaction with it, form our own behavior pattern, new way to respond.

Identifying the situation and our emotional reaction, next it's important to notice the thoughts born in response to it, that is "What do I think about this?", to notice how those thoughts trigger subsequent emotions.

For example, you're afraid of flying and you get on a plane, you feel anxious, and vegetative symptoms of anxiety start to arise, which are natural. But instead of understanding, accepting, enduring this state for further transformation, catastrophic thoughts and fantasies occur, causing you to scare yourself. This way, you fixate this reaction and repeatedly respond to similar situations in the same manner.

To cope with such states, you need to notice when catastrophic thoughts are born, understand what emotions they cause, and choose what to do about it in order to cope with it.

Sequence of emotion recognition:

Situation	**Thoughts**	**Feelings**	**Actions**
What happened?	What am I thinking?	What am I feeling?	What am I doing?

You need to practice keeping such records for two weeks. You will start to notice which emotions and thoughts prevail: feelings of guilt, anger, shame, anxiety.

And to deal with this, you need to pay attention to the thoughts you've recorded. Then it would become clear why this feeling prevails and what to do about it.

For example, if you feel scared, anxious (**feelings**), ask yourself: "What happened the day before, what is happening now, or what is about to happen?". You remember that you have an important conversation coming up (**situation**), and your thoughts about it are: "They won't understand me, they'll reject me, they won't accept me, they'll ridicule me" (**thoughts**). As a result, you choose to avoid this conversation (**actions**).

When you identify the thoughts that are running through your mind, it becomes clear why you feel anxious – it's the fantasies about being rejected.

Then you ask yourself: "Why do I think this way? How do I know that this person will reject me? Perhaps this reminds me of something from my childhood or past experiences?"

And then images from the past start to surface in your mind, like times when, in conversations with a close or significant person, you were rejected, ridiculed, or ignored. The outcome is that painful memories are transferred to the present and future; you fear that everything will repeat itself and you will feel pain again.

Based on your past experiences, and having no other experiences to draw from, you make conclusions about the future, second guess, fantasize, and act accordingly.

This all happens subconsciously, but if you start to track and recognize it, you can change your reaction. Thus, you discover that it is often these very thoughts that scare you; they are automatic and have already become ingrained, but now you know the true, deeper reason for your worries.

I'll give you another example: you wrote in the section **"feelings"** – indifference, emptiness. Start by following the thread back to the event that led to this state – you need to return to the moment after which you sank into indifference or emptiness. Here you discover that it happened after an argument with your partner (**situation**). You turned around and left (**action**), and your thoughts were: "He/She didn't even listen to me, it's the same thing again! How long can this go on?" (**thoughts**). Now think: do these thoughts correspond to your state? Or am I suppressing something, forbidding myself to feel?

My thoughts seem more like anger rather than emptiness and indifference, which means I am suppressing my anger!

Tuning into your body and your thoughts, you need to recognize whether your senses correspond with your thoughts and the situation.

If you notice that you are suppressing or forbidding certain emotions, pay even more attention to them. Remember when you learned to do this? Who taught you to do it? How helpful is it for you, and is it relevant now?

To navigate this process with ease, daily practice and effort are needed, as you have thought and reacted in one way your entire life. Now, you need to reconsider and rebuild that entire structure.

Now let's take a look at the feeling of **guilt.** Your friend complains to you about a lack of money (**situation**). After this conversation, you feel a pleasant sensation and start to focus on your senses, realizing that you experience guilt (**feelings**). Your thoughts are: "You're selfish, only thinking about yourself, you should help others, and if you don't help, no one will help you in trouble; what will people think of you?" (**thoughts**). And despite the fact that you are short of money or that this friend only reaches out to you when he/she needs help, under the pressure of guilt, you still call and offer your help (**action**).

Pay attention to your thoughts: who told you something like this before? Or who did you hear this from?

At that moment, you might remember that your parents used to say things like this, rebuking you and putting pressure on your feeling of guilt when you didn't fulfil their requests. You then understood that you had to do things you didn't even want to do, or else they would stop loving you, you wouldn't be able to ask for help, they would turn away from you, punish you, shame you.

Now, in adult life, the same voice still haunts you, and you don't even doubt it's right because you've never wondered where that voice came from in your head or why you think that way.

Next, we will talk about the mindsets and beliefs that are currently taking control over you.

Anger. If you notice that you often write about feelings of irritation, anger, dissatisfaction, or hatred in your journal, you should also analyze your thoughts during this state.

Let's take this situation: your husband doesn't help you with the cleaning, or your wife doesn't tidy up the house (**situation**). This makes you angry (**feeling**), and thoughts swirl in your head: "He/She is bad, never helps me, does nothing for the family, doesn't think about me, doesn't love me, how infuriating he/she is!" (**thoughts**). You burst into the room and start shouting (**actions**).

What should you pay attention to? First of all, take a second look at yourself and think whether your behavior reminds you of something you observed in childhood, for example. Perhaps your mom or dad acted in the same way, shouting, arguing, and using the words that now swirl in your head?

You may have learned this behavior and reaction from them, but now that you've recognized it, you can stop doing this and learn to express your emotions in a healthier way.

Let's also consider **shame.** You are probably familiar with situations where you chose not to do something, not to go somewhere, or not to say something precisely because you felt shame. This shame arose from your thoughts that you can't do anything, that you're nothing, stupid, unattractive, uninteresting, unnecessary, and that you always make mistakes.

And here we come to the issue of our negative beliefs about ourselves. Ask yourself: "Why do I see myself this way? Who called me that, who said this to me?". You will likely come to realization that in childhood, you were often shamed and insulted, and in your teenage years, for example, when you confessed your love to a boy or girl, you were ridiculed and rejected.

There can be many such situations, though even one is enough to form similar beliefs about yourself. Now these beliefs govern you, where oppressive thoughts are born, influencing your behavior.

We've described the emotions of anger, shame, guilt, and anxiety, which most often manifest throughout the day. Meanwhile, emotions like joy, interest, tenderness, and excitement can be ignored or devalued. That's why it's so important to notice them as well; you can rely on these emotions when making decisions.

Joy and interest, as you already know, tell us what we like, which direction to move in, who to bond with, and what to do. By noticing and recognizing the full spectrum of your emotions, your task is to process each one without fixating on just one, not intensifying any particular feeling, but instead mastering various states.

Remember the situations that bring you pleasant sensations, the people you enjoy being with, the activities that inspire you, and now, consciously try to choose them, create them, and strive for them.

This is not about which emotions you should experience and which you shouldn't; it's about living your life wholly and consciously. And by

EMOTIONS: AN INSTRUCTION MANUAL

orienting yourself to various life situations, emotions, sensations, you could choose what you want the most and what you like more.

Task for recognizing emotions:

For 1-2 weeks write in your journal about situations, thoughts, emotions, and actions as we learned in this chapter.

The point is for you to learn to trace the cause-and-effect link.

Situation	Thoughts	Feelings	Actions
What happened?	What am I thinking?	What am I feeling?	What am I doing?

CHAPTER 5
HOW TO EXPRESS YOUR EMOTIONS?

When we don't express our emotions but choose to hold them back, "swallow", replace them with another emotion, or devalue them, we must understand that our organism doesn't stop functioning. It immediately responds to the stimulus and initiates the appropriate process to prepare us for certain actions.

For example, if someone treats you roughly, your brain interprets it as a threat, you start to feel angry and in order to protect yourself, adrenaline is released into your bloodstream, and you are prepared for a "fight or flight" response. However, you have a restriction on expressing anger or want to maintain the relationship, and you don't know how to express your rage otherwise, you choose to suppress it.

Meanwhile, in your head, you keep replaying what you would like to do, say, which means your organism remains tense. As a result, you become exhausted, accumulating more and more; this knot grows larger and you become exhausted again because it takes a tremendous amount of psychic energy to contain it. You become irritated by every little thing, and at some point, you explode like a bomb or become seriously ill, as the body internalizes suppressed emotions.

By being able to express and process each emotion, you free yourself from it.

In order to build relationships, it is essential to have the skill of expressing emotions. This way, we show and communicate to the other person what behavior towards us is acceptable and what is not, providing him/her with feedback on his/her behavior. Ultimately, we learn to interact with each other in a way that makes us comfortable in these relationships.

One of the most important rules is to express emotions timely to avoid "exploding" later. You are deceiving yourself if you think that by holding back an emotion, you are controlling it and that it won't disturb you anymore. Remember that sooner or later, the emotion will find a way out, but how and to what extent will be revealed over time.

By hiding any existing emotions in a relationship – whether it's joy or anger – you increase the distance between each other, and this is not about closeness. You didn't express your emotion, the person didn't understand you, you became even more offended, and as a result, you closed yourself off.

Closeness is when you can naturally manifest yourself and know that you won't be rejected, that you can have a disagreement but then discuss it and become even closer. You can show your childlike side, genuinely rejoice, knowing that you won't be ridiculed but supported.

We can express emotions nonverbally, verbally, and through actions.

Nonverbal way includes our gestures, facial expressions, tone of voice, and posture.

So, when we nonverbally express anger – our voice becomes harsher, our eyebrows furrow, our jaw tightens – while at the same time saying, "Everything is fine, I'm not angry", our conversation partner understands, either consciously or subconsciously, that we are being insincere. This elicits a counter response – anger, offence, fear, and so on.

But it can also be the opposite: you want to protect yourself and your personal boundaries, saying "Don't do that anymore, I'm angry", while your face, voice and posture do not express anger but rather fear – wide eyes, hunched shoulders, a trembling or quiet voice. In this case, your conversation partner reads this and does not take your words seriously.

Or there's another option: you express your offence nonverbally but do not want to articulate or explain what happened, expecting the other person will read your mind and understand everything on his/her own.

But this way also does not give the desired result – we do not satisfy our needs. And even if the other person manages to figure it out, relationships in which people manipulate each other and have to guess what the other is thinking will not be strong or happy.

Verbal way refers to our words, the most powerful tool for expressing emotions!

Precisely thanks to speech we can fully, clearly, and distinctly tell about ourself, our worries, and our desires.

When we articulate to others what we like and what we don't, they will be able to understand us.

You should constantly talk about your feelings honestly and openly, broadcast your inner world to others. This way, you take responsibility for your emotions, putting them out into the space, while other people are responsible for their own reactions to your emotions.

Everything is clear: you give others a chance to understand you as much as possible, while also gaining the chance to be heard.

You should speak in a nonviolent manner, meaning not to make claims, not to shout, panic, attack, insult, but to **talk** about your feelings using "I" statements.

- "I" Statement means speaking on your behalf, from your "I". It's not "You make me angry", but "I feel angry when this happens". It's not "You offend me", but "I feel offended".
- When you start using "you" statements, the conversation partner starts defending himself/herself and no longer thinking about how to understand you.
- Speak only for yourself; don't try to assert anything on behalf of the other person. It sounds like this: "When you do that, I feel angry, irritated, and a lot of fury arises in me. Please don't do that to me anymore, okay?".
- Describe your body sensations, thoughts, and emotions as fully as possible, just as you do in your journal.
- Clearly explain what event triggers these worries for you, describe why, and how you would like things to be.
- Listen to your partner while continuing to track your own sensations. Perhaps response you hear may intensify or, conversely, calm them; articulate these changes as well: "I am calming down now, I'm feeling better", or "I am getting even angrier, these words make me uncomfortable".
- Broadcast about your state to the other person in as much detail as possible, so that he/she understands the direction to take,

and you continue to recognize what is happening.
- Remember how we learned to analyze the similarity of the situation with past events. Share with your partner a childhood experience that comes to mind and intensifies your feelings in the present moment; this will help you become closer and move to a deeper level of understanding.
- Articulate your thoughts, also relying on yourself: "I feel like you don't love me, and when I think that way, I become very sad".
- Notice how the statement is emotionally rich, articulated from an "I" perspective, without claims or attack. You have simultaneously expressed your thoughts and feelings fully without attacking the other person.
- If there are beliefs in your mind that have formed "secondary emotions", articulate those as well.
-

For example, "I feel ashamed right now for being angry at you or for crying". Remember who made you feel ashamed of these emotions and recognize that these inculcations are now preventing you from expressing and processing your emotions freely. However, by articulating this now, you have the opportunity to receive support from your partner, allowing you to gain new experience – that what you are experiencing is not shameful, not bad, but natural and normal, and you have the right to do it.

It is always better to ask the other person than not to ask at all; this way, you will either receive confirmation or refutation of your assumptions.

There is nothing wrong if the other person replies, "I don't want to talk about this", or "Yes, that makes me angry about you". This way, you can adjust and regulate your own behavior.

It's important to distinguish between constructive criticism, which is a nonviolent attitude toward you, and when someone is constantly trying to humiliate, suppress, or reject you.

When a person tells this with the desire of improving your relationship and being honest and open with you, versus when it's said or done to mould and control you.

We have many beliefs and prejudices about our emotions:

"If I ask for help, then I'm weak"
"If I get angry, then I'm bad"
"If I cry, then I'm "doormat"
"If I show tenderness, then I'm vulnerable"
"If I get too joyful, then I'll end up crying bitterly"
"If I open up and show my true self, then I'll be rejected"
"If I talk about my feelings, I'll bore the other person"
"If I praise someone else, they'll become conceited"
"If I praise myself, I'll become conceited"
"If I talk about my desires, then I'm selfish"
"If I show love, then I'll be abandoned"

Remember that all of this was once instilled in us by others, and now it seems to us that it is the truth.

It's time to reconsider these beliefs and bring in question them.

As long as you think based on this worldview, the people and events in your life will correspond to and confirm it. However, once you decide to expand your perception, to view everything differently, and are ready to accept new experience, this worldview will change.

When you learn to express your emotions as described above, you'll need to get used to it, which requires consistent practice. You need to form a new skill by repeating what you've learned over and over again.

Therefore, if you talked to someone like that once and he/she didn't hear you, it's no reason to break down and revert to your usual pattern.

What you do is for yourself, for your life, not for others; how others respond is their business, their responsibility.

Take responsibility only for yourself, for your words, behavior, and actions. If you've decided to change your pattern, then work on it without expecting others to change and everything to be the way you want.

Be ready to listen to and hear others, their thoughts and emotions. Apply the same strategy of recognition and identifying emotions: ask the conversation partner what he/she feels and why, what he/she thinks, what he/she wants, pay attention to his/her physical reactions, voice, facial expressions, and gestures.

Recognizing your emotions, you should understand what need they express or protect.

If you feel angry when someone enters your room without knocking, takes your things, or advises you on what to do, it indicates a need for personal space and respect for your boundaries.

If you feel angry that you are doing all household chores by yourself, it means you have a need for help and support.

If you fear being rejected, it means you have a need to be accepted.

When you recognize your need or desire, you can confidently state it: "I want...".

If you are just squabbling and expressing your emotions but don't know what for, what your goal is, or what you want, the results may not satisfy you.

You will need to state what need you want to be satisfied or protected and **ask** for it.

After your conversation, time has passed, and you notice that your requests are still being ignored, try to repeat the conversation and say that you see your requests are being ignored, and why?

Explain that if this continues, you will end the relationship or there will be other unpleasant consequences.

If that doesn't help either, then follow through with what you warned.

You can express emotions through actions.

When our actions speak for themselves, for example, we leave when we feel uncomfortable to be here, or we hug when we feel tenderness. Actions can either correspond with our words and thoughts, or not. Therefore, all three ways of expressing emotions – nonverbal, verbal, and through actions – should correspond with each other and to be implemented evenly.

Now let's specifically look at how to express anger, anxiety, shame and guilt, disgust, and sadness.

Anger:

1) List the facts that you don't like.
2) Tell that this makes you angry.
3) Identify and tell what need is being violated.
4) Make a clear request for what you want.
5) State the consequences.

Physical expression:

You can direct this energy into sports, go for a run, take a walk, turn on music and dance, sing, draw, hit a pillow, hit a punching bag, write an angry letter and burn it, go to a shooting range, or head out to a field or forest and shout for a while.

There are many alternative ways; the point of these methods is to relieve muscle tension, and they should be dynamic.

Shame and guilt:

1) Try not to physically tense up.
2) Articulate that you feel guilty or ashamed right now.
3) If your feelings of guilt and shame are rational, meaning they have real, objective reasons, then apologize.
4) If they are irrational, meaning you've second-guessed others, or have fallen into trauma, then change your thinking (work with thoughts is described in previous chapters).

Anxiety, fear:

1) Articulate that you are afraid or worried.

Disgust:

1) Express it through actions – leave or change the situation.
You should not tolerate what is aversive to you.

Sadness:

1) Tell that you feel sad.
2) Cry, be silent, or share your feelings.
3) Ask for support.

It is equally important to articulate and express all other emotions through actions.

Allow yourself to show tenderness, joy, and love:
"I miss you", "I love you", "I really like talking to you", "I feel so good being next to you", "You are so beautiful", "You are so talented", "You did a great job!".

Living life to the fullest means sensing its wholeness and value, and we can do this through our emotions and feelings. Don't strive to get rid of so-called negative emotions by merely thinking "positively" – this is self-deception. Instead, focus on your thinking, the reasons behind it, and your patterns of response.

The point is to be able to manage your emotions, rather than trying to eliminate those you can't cope with.

To manage means to know how to recognize and process them.

Task: write down your beliefs about feelings and emotions, about how you and others should behave, what you should or shouldn't experience, which emotions are "good" and which are "bad".

Everything that are your principles, rules, obligations, and reasoning. Examples of such beliefs were listed earlier in this chapter.

Ask these beliefs the following questions:
- Who told me this?
- The person who told me this, what was the basis for his/her conclusion?
- How competent is this person in this matter?
- Was this conclusion drawn from one or several cases?
- Has it ever been or can it be different?
- How relevant is this belief to me now?
- Do I personally agree with it? Do I feel comfortable following it?

Challenge each point if they no longer feel relevant or cause discomfort, and formulate new beliefs.

In the future, whenever you hear that familiar voice with old beliefs, activate your new ones. Repeat them as many times as necessary until you start to feel confident.

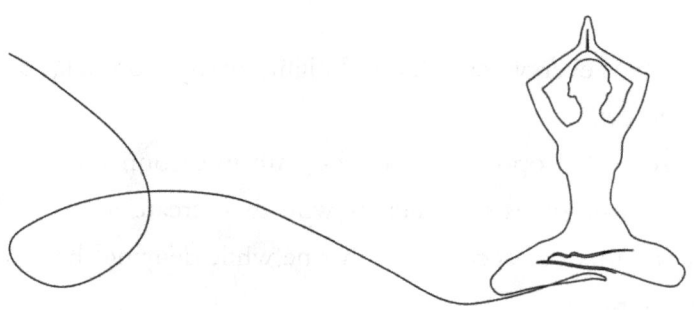

CHAPTER 6
CONSCIOUS PROCESSING OF EMOTIONS

We have learned fundamental skills of emotional self-regulation and have even delved deeper into the connection between childhood, past painful experience, and our "today".

Now I want to introduce you to a higher level of self-mastery and mastery of own state.

Let's start by reconsidering the concept of "bad" and "good" feelings. Yes, it's quite convenient to make this distinction to know what to do and what not to do, how to be and how NOT to be... We automatically try to eliminate everything "bad", and by naming any emotion as "bad", we deprive it the right to exist, which means we also deprive the right for a part of ourselves to exist.

It doesn't work that way that you have just decided not to feel something, pushing it aside, and living on perfectly and carefree.

In this way you deny yourself, fragment and lose touch with your Essence, with your nature.

You don't need to break yourself down, but to bring yourself together.

Duality is everywhere: day and night, heaven and hell, love and hate, good and evil.

These are all opposites, but they are interconnected. Without one, the other cannot exist, which is why they create a whole. Therefore, separating them or accepting only one while denying the other destroys the whole picture.

It's the same with you and me, we're made of opposites.

We are kind as well as angry, we love as much as we hate, and we are innocent as well as guilty.

However, it sometimes seems that if we fight against our shadow side and defeat it, we can free ourselves from suffering. If we try to erase memories, offences, rage, we will become happier. But everything that has been is a part of you. You should graciously accept all the pieces of yourself, connecting them, and finding your Whole Self, stepping on the path that leads to your own Essence.

Do not breed war in yourselves, strive for peace.

After all, it's a vicious cycle: we don't like that we are angry at someone or something, and we start getting angry with ourselves for feeling that way – anger doesn't go away; it just takes on a more sophisticated form.

Although our reactions, including anger, are natural, they deserve to exist; we shouldn't be ashamed of them or lock them away in a closet, allowing them to transform into monsters that devour our souls.

All our feelings can transform and take on a different flavor if we accept them.

Do not renounce Yourself, do not fight against Yourself – come to an agreement, accept.

You have the right to feel any emotion, and it's better to give it the freedom to be expressed. When given the chance to be expressed, their manifestation won't be so destructive.

Thus, I suggest you erase rigid, black-and-white boundaries and start to see each feeling as a distinct, whole, and important phenomenon, as energy.

What we call suffering is energy.
What we call happiness is energy.
Every feeling, emotion, and state is energy.

We label it, naming It, and then classify it as a "bad" or "good" emotion...

What do we end up with? "I feel sad – sadness is bad – I'm feeling bad".

If we remove these labels and classifications, what remains is Energy, which has taken on this form for now; just like a thought, it will live its time and be replaced by another.

By resisting "bad" emotions and feelings – rage, fear, suffering – we experience discomfort, and the turmoil accelerates: "I urgently need to get rid of this! This is bad... it's not normal; it shouldn't be this way, I don't want to experience this, I can't stand it. Why is it like this? There should be happiness, happiness is good".

And many such thoughts of resistance to certain forms of Energy.
Everything you sense has a right to exist; suffering lives just as

happiness does. Allow yourself to BE in these energies, to process them, rather than hiding them away in the depths in the hope that they will never return. By holding them back, blockages are happening. It is the process of fully processing these emotions until the point of bifurcation (the critical state after which state transformation happens) that grants them release, allowing the flow to continue.

We just keep running from corner to corner, trying to avoid "bad" emotions, seeking endless harmony and thinking that it is possible to structure chaos... I don't see harmony in this turmoil; I see hurly burly.

Stop in the middle, then erase that boundary and sense the infinity and simultaneity of the processes that have been, are, and will be. We are the ones who give them names; we create them as they are... Remove the label, don't give it a designation, and feel what that is like.

This is about responsibility — we are the creators of our own senses; each worry is born within us, not in someone else or outwardly. Recognizing this gives you the understanding that the control panel is in your hands.

It is a very important skill to be able not to be equated with every thought in your head, every emotion, or every event.

In other words, to be an Observer. This practice should begin after you have learned to identify, recognize, and express your emotions.

Observer watches from a distance. Imagine that you are observing a one or another thought or emotion from a distance; you examine its form, its content, and notice its beginning, culmination, and ending. You observe its life cycle.

Exercise: remember a recent experience and re-create it. Now imagine how you yourself create this emotion: what form does it take, color, its content?

Pay attention on your breathing; breathe deeply and steadily while continuing to observe this energy. Try not to assess or name it, and do not reject or accept it – just let it be.

Learn to accept every manifestation of yourself and life, to respond consciously, and to notice and observe.

The next level of observation is to observe yourself as the one observing the emotion, or as the one going through that emotion.

I want to emphasize the significance of the saying "going through"; it is about an emotion has its own "life" and that you are going through it.

It is very important to fully process the emotion, allowing it to hang around for the necessary, normal amount of time without interfering or resisting, but rather observing.

While processing, remember to breathe; do not hold your breath. Take steady, rhythmic inhales and exhales, as if moving in a circle with smooth transitions.

As you observe yourself from a different perspective, do not strive to control what is happening. Your task is to learn to observe.

Remember that every phenomenon in this life, every state is not infinite, everything has an end, everything goes.

When you are able to stop resisting certain emotions, you will understand what it means to process them.

If you interfere in its life cycle, it gets stuck in you and becomes your burden. Learn to accept each of your worries with gratitude; they exist now, but soon they will be gone, replaced by another, just like thoughts.

Exercise: pay attention to your own thoughts. Notice how one thought replaces another and space between them.

Just as one thought replaces another, our emotions also change. As soon as you decide to control a thought or an emotion, it becomes heavier and stops; its natural flow slows down.

Listen to your body – it holds all the answers.

If you are honest with yourself and possess the skill to recognize causes and effects, you are able to draw resources from within yourself to process various states.

Trust the spontaneous movements of your body: if you are emotionally in pain, turn to your body and listen to what it needs to help you in that moment.

If you feel inspired, turn to your body and listen to what you want to create and how to do it.

Try not to bypass or run away from any emotion and thought, they will pass. If you don't process your emotions, they will remain within you.

For example, if you want to bypass sadness and to be in the moment where you're already having fun, you end up rejecting your own energy that naturally occurs in response to an event and helps you complete the cycle, allowing another emotion to appear in the same natural way.

If you'd constantly rewound a movie and only watched it in fragments, it would end for you very quickly, and afterward, you wouldn't feel the wholeness of what you've seen, and as a result, you wouldn't feel satisfied.

So, for conscious processing, you need to:

1) Take responsibility for creating your own states.

2) Become an Observer of your thoughts and emotions: visualize their form, content, and life cycle without assessing or giving names to them.

3) Pay attention to your breath: steady, full, and continuous.

4) Become an Observer of yourself, observing your thoughts and emotions.

5) Do not resist.

6) Listen to your body.

7) Remember that one state always replaces another.

8) Be in the here and now.

Regarding the last point, I want you to understand that life is happening not in the past or the future, but only "now". By running back or rushing ahead, you miss the living moment that you can truly process.

With the past you create already past states, it is necessary only to finish processing them and releasing them.

Thinking about what you will feel in the future is merely a sum of your past experiences and your relevant worries right now. You know how it will be, but you remember how it was and understand how it is now. This is where you need to concentrate, as you can only make changes in the present moment, not in a fantastical future.

Let's take a particular example of what it means to process:

Shame and guilt.

It's important to analyze guilt and identify whether it is rational or not.

Rational guilt is when there are presented objective facts that you caused the other person harm.

For example, when you broke your friend's favorite vase in her house or forgot to wish someone close to you a happy birthday.

That kind of guilt has a real justification.

Irrational is when you think you've done something bad, you second guess others and plot a catastrophic scenario in your head.

For example, children often feel guilty about their parents' divorce, even though, in fact, they had nothing to do with it. Similarly, when guilt peaks and disproportionate to the action – like saying something thoughtless yet blaming yourself as if you've committed a serious crime.

In the first case, you need to process rational guilt through repentance. This means you don't deny or resist it; instead, you acknowledge the reasons and allow yourself to sit with that feeling, so guilt can transform into self-forgiveness.

Confess and ask the person you feel guilty about for forgiveness or, if possible, make an effort to fix the situation.

When the situation cannot be fixed, you need to work on your desire to control. Confess to yourself that you want to control life and the events in it, then recognize that this is impossible and process your feeling of helplessness and powerlessness, and share your worries with someone you trust.

In the second case, you need to work on cognitive distortions by reconsidering and analyzing the situation from a different perspective, whether you truly caused harm to another person and if what you did was really as terrible as you believe.

If you understand that guilt is toxic, you need to learn not to act under its influence. Recognize that your thoughts are irrational, and you need to work to develop a new response to them.

In this book, we won't delve into the work on irrational guilt; our current goal is to understand what it means to process.

Shame can also be rational or toxic. It's important to learn how to allow it pass through yourself by confessing to yourself that you feel ashamed, especially if you have genuinely done something that crosses reasonable boundaries. "Yes, I did this, I am in this state right now, I breathe and endure". If necessary, apologize or change the situation. Don't avoid it, take responsibility for what happened, don't exacerbate or "condense" it – just allow that feeling to be.

Anger.

"I am very angry right now, there is a lot of anger within me". Breathe and allow yourself to feel angry, observing this emotion from a distance as it changes and transforms. Recognize "There is me, and there is anger", rather than "I am anger". Notice the thoughts that support this state without being equated to them.

Example: "This world is unfair, everything is against me, I'm so annoyed by everyone, I hate it!".

Don't resist these thoughts; let them pass. Observe them from a distance, gradually shifting your focus to other thoughts that can help cool down that anger.

In this case, it's also important to work on cognitive distortions. If you hold beliefs that everyone is against you, that everyone is evil and wants to harm you, you will react disproportionately even to minor stimuli.

Fear.

Confess to yourself that you are scared; you have fears and that's normal, you have the right to feel this way. Allow fear to pass through you without being equated to it. There is fear, and there is me, recognize reasons.

Talk about your fear with others, breathe, observe its form and content. Notice those thoughts that you scare yourself with, without being equated to them. Watch how they appear and disappear.

Sadness.

Be sad, cry, mourn, if feeling has now occurred, let it hang around, let it go through its cycle.

Notice what is happening in your body, look at yourself and the situation from a distance, empathize and sympathize with yourself.

Recognize that this, too, shall pass, but this feeling is just as important and natural; don't resist it, let it come to a natural end. Notice the thoughts that exacerbate your state without being equated to them.

For example, there are such thoughts in your mind like, "No one will love me anymore, I won't meet anyone else, I will be lonely, I can't do anything, nothing will help me".

Allow these thoughts to hang around, recognizing that they are exaggerated at the moment. Be a compassionate and warm figure for yourself.

Joy.

Allow joy to flow through you; sense how it is filling you. Concentrate on the sensations in your body, breathe, and spread this feeling within, enjoy it, slow down.

Visualize joy, imagine it is born within you, share it with other people.

Don't try to hold it; recognize that it, too, will pass with time. Be present in the moment, don't rush into the future, and don't forbid yourself to experience it of fear that it will pass.

Yes, it will pass, but right now it exists, and I choose to be in it.

Allow it to come and go easily, letting it to live its natural cycle.

Interest.

Allow yourself to feel inspired, focus on your body, what is happening within it. Where does this interest born, and what do you want to do with it?

Observe its dynamics; feel, recognize that you may forbid yourself from experiencing it, but right now you choose to be in it. Tell about your interest to other people; don't resist or fear it. Instead, observe and study this energy as it fills you.

As you can see, the principle is the same — don't resist and be in it.

Remember that resistance creates even greater discomfort, and you get stuck in it.

Full processing liberates and supports the natural cycle of life.

In stressful situations, you may find yourself lacking mental strength, and you will react as you usually do. But know this, it is normal, natural. If this happens, accept it. And when you feel ready to respond differently, go ahead and do so.

Afterword

Now you possess the knowledge and skills to understand yourself and manage your state. However, remember that to develop a new behavior pattern, you need to practice consistently and put in the effort. Continue to pay attention to your body, breath, distinguish your emotions, ask yourself questions, trace the connections, state your desires, articulate your thoughts, and observe yourself from a distance.

These skills are indeed the foundation, a solid base for building the life you want.

Don't expect changes to happen very quickly, although that is possible. Everything has its own time, and each person has their own pace.

Continue to grow and discover yourself, be open to opportunities, and stay connected with both yourself and the world around you.

It takes a lifetime to work on yourself, as we are constantly changing, facing new, and learning to adapt to it.

Deeper delve into yourself and working-through require guidance from a specialist. Be careful and considerate of yourself, recognize your worth, and if something doesn't satisfy you, don't hesitate to make a change.

When there is a need, resources will follow. Your inaction is also a choice. The choice not to change and remain your own prisoner. By choosing to take action, you gain a wealth of emotional experiences and opportunities in this world!

A Workbook to Deepen Your Journey

Looking to put the lessons from *Emotions: An Instruction Manual* into action? The **Emotions Workbook** by Nioza Hubanova is the perfect companion to this book, designed to help you deepen your understanding and mastery of your emotions.

This practical guide includes exercises, worksheets, and prompts that will help you:

- **Recognize and track your emotions:** Daily and weekly exercises to help you identify patterns and triggers.
- **Develop emotional expression skills:** Step-by-step activities to practice expressing your feelings in healthy, constructive ways.
- **Strengthen emotional intelligence:** Interactive scenarios to help you improve how you manage emotions in various situations.
- **Build better relationships:** Exercises to enhance communication and connection with others through emotional clarity.

By working through the exercises, you'll move from understanding your emotions to living in harmony with them every day.

Available on Amazon!

www.ingramcontent.com/pod-product-compliance
Lightning Source LLC
Chambersburg PA
CBHW060347050426
42449CB00011B/2853